IMAGINARY MENAGERIE

Ailbhe Darcy was born in Dublin in 1981 and brought up there, and currently lives in South Bend, Indiana. She has published her poetry in Ireland, Britain and the US, and co-edits *Moloch*, an online magazine of new art and writing. Selections of her work are included in the recent Bloodaxe anthologies *Identity Parade* and *Voice Recognition*, and in her pamphlet *A Fictional Dress* (tall-lighthouse, 2009). *Imaginary Menagerie* (Bloodaxe Books, 2011) is her first book-length collection.

Ailbhe Darcy

IMAGINARY MENAGERIE

BLOODAXE BOOKS

ISBN: 978 1 85224 901 4

First published 2011 by
Bloodaxe Books Ltd,
Highgreen,
Tarset,
Northumberland NE48 1RP.

www.bloodaxebooks.com
For further information about Bloodaxe titles
please visit our website or write to
the above address for a catalogue.

Supported by
**ARTS COUNCIL
ENGLAND**

Cover design: Neil Astley & Pamela Robertson-Pearce.

Printed in Great Britain by
Bell & Bain Limited, Glasgow, Scotland.

for John Harvey

ACKNOWLEDGEMENTS

Acknowledgements are due to the editors of the following publications in which some of these poems, or versions of them, previously appeared: *Brittle Star, The Cortland Review, Drop Out, Identity Parade: New British and Irish Poets* (Bloodaxe Books, 2010), *nthposition, The Pem, Pomegranate, Salamander, Seam, The Stinging Fly, Voice Recognition: 21 Poets for the 21st Century* (Bloodaxe Books, 2009), *Watermarks,* and *The Wolf.* 'Swan Song' was commissioned by Benjamin Morris and Helen Mort for St George's Day 2009. Joyelle McSweeney gave me brilliant feedback on an early draft of the manuscript. Several of the poems appeared in my pamphlet *A Fictional Dress* (tall-lighthouse, 2009).

Thanks to Hesitancy Dargle for their album *Maigret Hesitates*, and to The National Prayer Breakfast for their albums *The Sociables Prefer Pop Music* and *This Is My Happening And It XXXXXX Me Up*. Thanks, Mum and Dad, Ness and Barr.

Putting together a first collection turns out to involve over a decade of conversation with – and encouragement from – generous and intelligent people. I've encountered too many to thank them all here. I hope you know who you are.

CONTENTS

Gone Fishing

War. And one fierce girl
will not take the bait.
She swims off to stop it,

leaves me dangling, thumb-sucking,
plucking patterns from tea leaves,
scanning advice slips from bank machines,
clutching at strings.

I'd swing
from the cat's cradle of clouds
crossing borderless skies
if I believed it would catch
and knit me
into any design;
I'd loop-the-loop,
crossing, recrossing truths.

But it all comes loose.
Nets become sieves,
knots become loops.
I feel that old slack,
no certainty to pull taut,
make sing, draw back
that girl-fish
or tightrope out and join her
stitched fast to a bridge
over the Tigris.

The mornings you turn into a grub

it begins with the heart.
You lie listening to the thunder
of bin men hoisting garbage larvae
from outside every house. Your housemate
showers, bangs things, jangles keys, moves
                                    away at a trot.

You feel your blood thickening,
slurring. You think of Henry Sugar,
able to self-diagnose. You warn the ceiling,
'I think I'm having a heart attack.' Your chest
seems to swell
or contract. You wonder
if you have woken as a fat, middle-aged man,
instead of beside one.

You feel all sclerotic. No, you feel soft.
You feel like a scrambled egg omelette,
having once read the recipe
in a Sunday supplement:
Edward de Bono's Jolly Good Eggs.
'Most omelette fillings,' wrote Ed,
'are boring and detract from the eggs.'

For this recipe you make the omelette as usual,
but before you fold it in two,
you fill up its belly with scrambled eggs.

The result is an omelette with an omelette taste
but a soft and runny interior. The taste
is pure egg all the way through. You are pure egg,
all the way through,
the mornings you turn into a grub.

Poles

When the Poles came to the National Gallery
I lowed at a painting by this Edward Okún,
and what I was thinking was that was me below
your drop-gemmed black coat all winter, wind
around us beating like wings, chests pressed together.
I had put down roots right there in the street
and told you this now is home and you
said now we can go anywhere. I hear now

that they're finished building Dublin up
the side of a mountain, the Poles have hied
home and put up signs: *No Irish*;
and no one blames them. A slow flight;
the old crone creeping; the cupped flower;
his wife looking at him and not around her.

Icon

The bibelot I brought you from Cluj Napoca
looms over our flat in South Bend, Indiana,
its feathered wings cocked like an antenna.

Being an icon, that bird or holyghost will always
deflect you back to the thing itself, the res,
the broad black tracks over which she hovers.

Pointing one quavered wing towards
Detroit, Chicago, Boston or New York,
along the Amtrak or the South Shore

line, she may supervise the hatted Amish
or tend to our own Thoreauvian insistence
on honest suffering's own sake in transit,

you and me. There are some crude flurries
of snow ranged around her in bristled threes,
the tern prints in snow of Groarke's fleeing

lines in 'Flight', or the three that exists
outside signs, in the still point amidst
them, making them shiver, the steam whistle,

the train tracks that shudder like a mirror
in its frame when the train passes, shuddering,
a house near the railway with a framed mirror

in it. Snow is always general in Ireland now;
it is also always ashes; it is the backdrop for roses.
And the same Romanian made the frame that encloses

the whole – of the icon, I mean – as if taking
full responsibility for the putting of this thing
into the world. It seems we also think,

you and me, that a life, two lives, lived deliberately,
carefully, might evade somehow the arbitrary,
the unintended pun, the rhyme that leads a line astray.

Three lives, maybe. What do we court
when we speak of pregnancy, to what
presiding gimmick could we pray for what

parents seek: a future, some struggling, some ease?
Would a child fear the creature was inclined to leave
the picture, the way it keels, its sheepish fleece?

We might have to answer that we were gazing
on the icon when our earth was blazing;
that the very care we took was a displacement

from the res. That the tchotchke I brought
you on the train from Cluj Napoca
was loaded all along, and cocked.

Telephone

(for Lady Gaga)

1

A cinema under the dome, cheap matinée seats,
and we have the whole show to ourselves. Pass the cookie dough.
The thriller is set on an island, in a storm of course, so that
the ferry is cancelled. And in the forties, not just for the Cold
War, psychotropic drugs, returning trauma of an aestheticised
Holocaust, but because now our hero, on the run in a world
shrunk so small one Hitler in it means mad days for all,
could phone a friend and squeal: Just get me out of here!
A little machine / which makes us able to say anything

2

It drops into my lap out of the ether,
a lightning bug crash-landed, its glow, chirp and stutter.
Lapsed on the couch, moon-faced by television,
it insists on me still, its peal, light and vibration;
'Pub?' the message ticks. Quick as that,
I'm in Dublin, I'm stung, wrapped up, stepped out, lit;
I'm light-stepping through the darkened park, I'm
careening down the hill to the village in the dark;
ordering, making the transaction, looking for the place to sit;
and raising a glass to yourself, for taking me out of myself.

3

What's given by the blast
is deep rain, an orgy of worms. Trees
shake their manes, each branch a business
of sexy division. Each bud has a drop for aureole
I *want* you to touch. Spring, and all
that.

We must have kissed a hundred times
in rain like this: I fell flat on my back
in a field; we waltzed about the fountain in that
Barcelona square, fought like
cats and dogs, and made up; or when I
dropped the bottle we were keeping
and it crashed a gloria of crimson rivulets.
You took me home, all the same.
                       All the same,
the blasting veteran on our bus home
wields his unbusy stump.
It never buds purple moles,
explodes wild carrot. It stays the same.

       That's why in your arms I sing
the man with a data drive embedded
where his finger was,
             a virtual place
where anyone can wield six
lobster claws,
       Max the robot cat, the device
you hold aloft when you don't know
what's playing
          on the jukebox, even
our ultimate uploading to the internet;
       and the world-altering pill
I take so that we make nothing
with our love,
       all these years,
only my crazy new hairdo,
wet and wild against a field of white pillow,
and the maddening blip of your phone,
a little machine
demanding to be plugged in again.

4

Say you'd barricaded the place,
sealed the exits, say the plot
was water tight. All the top bad
brass are in your theatre, you
projecting their doom. Your accomplice,
an altar server, holds his taper
to the stock, lighting the fuse.
Bad guy flambé! Let there be light!
And it is good.

Still, the call would come: a year
later, say, or two. In your kitchen, the man
you're with, chopping meat, would
hand you the phone: *it's for you-hoo!*
That's that: the late monster's voice deadpans,
crackling, rises to the shriek-bark; the little
moustache hopping, the knife slice, the
in one ear and out another,
the audience gasping.

5

Don't answer it. Don't
answer it, I want to say,
when the phone rings.

I want to speak with
your recorded voice,

for a predetermined
number of my minutes.

Market Square, Five Years After

1

On Market Square, six protestors sway in a line:
Don't attack Iran! Don't attack Iran!
Opening our hot baked potatoes to the air,
we laugh at them from our bench, sneer,
'we weren't going to.' We are no Cahun

and Moore. I am shamed when you remind me
of my five-years-ago self, suggest that the protest
I marched on then may not have stayed that war
but stopped this one. Is the world safer, then?
'No. It's not safer in Iraq' – Hans Blix.

2

Later I stand in the hotel shower
shampooing my soul over and over
because I'm worth it. When I step out
of the shower it's so quiet I wonder

if something has happened outside while we
were in here, if everyone has gone away to war
or died. We will troop out together
past the empty reception desk, the automatic

doors parting to enable passage,
the roads cleared of traffic. We can fill
our rucksacks with food from abandoned
stores, may have to move from hideout

to hideout, or start our own farm. When I step out
of the shower, you hold out your hand.
I drop the towel to shake it.

Clues

You are waiting at Derry with rain in your hair
to take me to St Columb's Cathedral
where Judas waits in turn
with soldiers and disruption.
A stone there sings:
They have raised a scarlet flag above my roof,
they have taken lead for shot
and bullets from my spire,
but egg-cups have been made of my ceiling wood!
It is singing and laughing
in the porch as we enter.

Walking pews carved with leaves,
I find you one lily baring its throat.
Gargoyle or sheela, its shape is less
the eye through which the rich cannot pass
than the seed of Parisian mecs
calling in the street,
Ta chatte!
or that of the Sistine Chapel brush stroke
that rendered of one cherub's gesture,
index and middle finger embracing a thumb,
an obscenity approaching Hallelujah.

And as you and I stitch up
naves with our footprints,
wind down giddy spires, pull faces
at great men in galleries,
or in eiderdown dens
unravel things we've seen or read,
ours is one long conversation
that supposes an answer.
We laugh at the idea. But then
you push a solving finger between my lips
and stone sings, boys shout, angels leer.

You had not looked

at that birch for years. Suddenly
betrayed, you took shears and
went at her.
With every thrust of blade
she would arch, shiver. Leaves
whispered prayers
or pleas.

Her sap tasted of some secret pleasure.
That of the apostle
erecting his own execution:
bent bough's long moan
following sob
of silver coins in cloth,
noose's embrace recalling
one sweet rebellious kiss
it is not. Who are you
to know such things? After,
you could not look at her.

Mrs Edgeway

She squeezed my waist between the
flats of her palms
like the obstacle to a prayer:
'so skinny!' her greeting.

          I had not seen her
since the wedding, when I dressed in green; she,
of course, in white. Everyone said
how young she was,
how decked-out in smiles.
                I was unsurprised.
She'd had her period in fourth class, breasts
before I knew to expect them. And now
she was displaying the weight
bestowed by marriage, as though
her husband was provider, fattened her
like a rich Ghanaian wife.
No child yet, but her belly ripe.

Later, I eye my body in the mirror:
not skinny. But hip bones
jut hard; between my breasts is a space
where the sky opens wide; my skin is translucent.
                  I trace the veins,
try to find some thing of substance.

Missives

Dave wrote that now you had stopped
smoking you drank a bottle of wine
instead of two in the evening.

And he wrote that the flesh on your body
had redistributed itself,
that you no longer had that little belly
now there was no stress. He seemed
to think it important.

Because nothing you tried to do seemed
to make any difference,
you went up into the mountains
where a baby donkey had been turned into a rock.

Beneath your feet was felt; trees
swaddled in climbing plants;
your teeth softened; billy busters
hung larvae from the hedge;
those berries you picked and filled
the punnets with were not sloe,

lacking the sheen. Dave writes
that there's more room in Whelan's these nights,
that Camden Street is sadder and wiser generally,
though there's still never an empty taxi.

But I'd swear I saw the soles of your feet
kicking up Grafton Street the other morning
and they were painted scarlet.

Two flares, flashing everyone in your thrall.

Breakfast with Braden

You put on your hat like a prop; nothing is yours
but the spotlight you stand up in. You've been up
all night again, playing card games with angels,
glancing off gin-traps, tasting the stakes. You're afraid

someone is dreaming this room and revealing
your secrets. You brew some black goo, stove
in the arses of eggshells for witches, turn
one Lucky Strike around in its box. You twitch

like peeling wax or glue from your fingers, your eyes
Baghdad Zoo. You can't read the papers; tears
humiliate you. So you're hunkering down for the day
in my kitchen, flirting, averting my questions:

it won't do. *You're the one-eyed jack in this town*, Mr
Braden, *but I seen the other side of your face.*

Dublin Opsimath

If a new start can be made
in an old place
this should do fine.
City of broken clocks,

skyscape of cranes,
roads that give way,
houses that simply appear.
I lie awake, afraid

of the sleep walk that would bring
me, along paths that used to be,
across a new motorway.
Yet you would take my hand

and lead me every time
by different streets
to the same kissing-doorway.
Unformed habits

in their throes,
praiseach, the flowers that bloom
on a building site,
one last vision of colour.

I dream of you saying,
why try to square it?
Let things have their way

He tells me I have a strange relationship

with my city. As though I were something divorced
from the skin I'm in, could scrap or elope with
my own tattooed scapula, pouting belly, saddle curve
of his palm's kiss.

But here's the vein on my left wrist
fat as Liffey, my right skinny
lost Dodder; slit,
they run murky and thick
with city. My left breast
thingmote, my right sugarloaf,
my throat a high and narrow pane, frogged
and pointed like a lancet.

My country stretches from a ham's span
outside the pale to the top
of Parnell Street. I cannot leave.
It is a narrow, self-effacing swathe,
the shape of me –
enough scar to fret at, too close to desire or despise.
If Dublin is kicks in the shins, my shin
is its sweet spot, summer lunchtime Stephen's Green.

Christina's World

(after Andrew Wyeth)

Lacking the means or will to sound
she began dumbly running hands
over and over the ground, splayed
on the slope beneath that big house
at Killiney or Glencullen. Gaps

between her fingers and nails picked
up signals from a plantation of ants,
her left thumb flicked into a socket
that might have once coddled a hero's
eye, or been rendered a moment before

by her right thumb. Rubble was
stroked by the heel of her hand
into gaps and spiral patterns, grass
flattened: she was flattening out
a place, deaf to a bass line of riders

approaching, or any salt of troubles
on the breeze. Anyway, she could
not dig a tunnel to escape her away;
she could not unearth treasure to pay
her passage; nor could she plumb

for truth: behind her is that view
of the whole of Dublin and the sea.
She hugs the slant land closer and
begins crawling to the next space, side-
ways, crabby-wise, elbows and knees.

Animal Biscuits

September 11 changed him, Alexie says, by revealing the 'end game of tribalism – when you become so identified with only one thing, one tribe, that other people are just metaphors to you'.
– from an interview with SHERMAN ALEXIE in the *Guardian*, May 2008

In the photograph you flaunt all your teeth
to signal you are not grown unwholesome
by the violence you do in the photograph.

You are hazing an Iraqi, working towards the Führer,
behaving as animals, violently absent from

your own photograph. When they took your picture
to court they constrained it in a chained
iron case, digital, weighty, flanked

by blank doormen; still, every morning here
on Colfax a squirrel spills out of a tree

onto gravel to wrench me awake.
Red. Not as the breast of the figure for bird
on a peaceably secular Christmas card,

not a scarlet alpha forcibly worked
onto a fictional dress, not the only colour

in a black and white film about war,
not even the real red dress,
belted, brief, minatory,

my daughter starved herself a week to wear;
not stripes, not love, not blood,

a squirrel will always dance clear.
And now there is a constellation of photographs
describing an animal we cannot dub archer or bear,

a creature we may not tame with metaphor
since metaphor got us into this mess.

But Alice is baking biscuits, she has eyes
like animals, her hands do not shake,
biscuits with nuts in, biscuits with butter,

each careful measure of what Alice adds.

Aus der Mappe der Hundigkeit

September fourteenth. Stopped by an image in the *New York Times*.
It is Valie Export's *Aus der Mappe der Hundigkeit*
(From the Portfolio of Doggedness), 1968.

A caption reads: *The artist walks a man like a dog*
through Vienna on a leash. It's from a show
stopping at the Bronx Museum of the Arts.

I scare you over breakfast, baying,
Was this funny before Abu Ghraib! Passers-by
stop to watch, in the photograph.

Something is rolling over in my head
and I want to stop it. A tale
from *Anne Frank* or *Hitler Stole Pink Rabbit*?

Older now, wise to imagination's tricks,
I want you to stop stopping your mouth with toast and speak,
to make the story better, without my having to tell it:

It's about a man, a Jew, tied up
outside the camp and scratch scratch
bark bark ruff ruff ruff ruff

La rue est rentrée dans la chambre

Last night when you clamped your hand
over my sex
I thought for a moment there was blood
on your hand.
I had seen hands performing bloody acts
on cable that day
that looked not unlike yours,
and thought you meant your hand to silence me.

When you arrested my skin inch by inch
with your mouth
I froze for a moment you'd taste sweat
on my skin.
I had read accusations of inaction
in the papers that day
that all but spelled out my name,
and thought myself a crime against humanity.

If we faced each other then, and pulled
each other to each other
was there too much between our skins
for us to have come?
That day we had watched bodies degraded
in mixed media, glorious
technicolor, all tongues
and none, and now I do not know if I am free.

Dog Song

1

Sing loud big cocked dog
The moon has cheese in its ears
End with a whimper
The universe answers thus
W-A-L-K-I-E-S

2

Met a dog
beneath a dollfaced moon:
It was only hair made him bigger
than my problems

Dg, I sd, I know a dog song,
I know some blue moon blues
shall we sing along together? So
we wagged & moseyed as one

cucka choo choo

only he had four legs
and gone over the horizon
twice as fast as I
had a hope to

Halo

It was late last night the dog was speaking of me,
and the gulls speaking of me, out over the field.
You were drawing water from the tap in the kitchen
and a moth was speaking of me, beating for light.

I was raising delft from the sink to the aumbry,
while they spoke of you in loops, over the waves.
I reached for a switch; sunlight coalesced
about your reflection, helmet of bright coils.

Outdoors was a blankness peopled with black angles;
waiting for the water you caught your own glance.
My eyebrows bustled, you submersed in my dress;
then you were speaking of me, just a word, in response.

All the dogs in America have sisters of their own,
all the birds have sisters, out on the highway.
Moths have moths for sisters, beating out for light,
and I am speaking of you here, to everyone I meet.

Stump

When we play Stump in Ethan's backyard,
a game come Midwest from Louisiana
in which one repeatedly casts a hammer
towards heaven and grasps it, I wonder
how real are all our lives.

Oh, the trappings are adequate real:
the hammer solid as a rudder,
the nails bought at a real nail shop,
the stump heavy plenty that three
of the girls grazed knees

lumbering it into the trunk of a car
in shorts, legs stocky with the prolonged
South Bend winter, our bottles of beer
the champagne of beers, weak American beer
we'd scoff at back home in Dundrum,

now the only beer for a long day's drinking
and playing Stump under South Bend sun.
But the trick for throwing the hammer
and catching it is counter to sensical,
and as the day rolls over, fattening,

no one suggests we should stop there
and re-enter our lives or use the hammer
to put up shelves or bash out the brains
of trespassers. And what is more,
we almost always catch it: *Whump*.

Socks

*The inherent unfinishedness and unpredictability of language –
the fact that I can never deduce from any two of your words
what the third one is going to be – is a token of human freedom,
and thus in a broad sense political.*

TERRY EAGLETON

I wear my socks odd, queer
bags a couple of feet from my

knees. I've heard that's how

the first dykes snagged the fair
sex: maybe some night I'll catch a feel.

Be honest, for that I wear my socks

spotted, freckled with eyes, crossed
all my t's as a young thing. I wear

my socks beneath my boots, where

they can't be seen. On very cold days
I wear my socks twice, and over my

tights, but always odd. I believe

that's right – the way you can't tell
what colour my knickers will be.

Shoes

(for Muntazer al-Zaidi)

Duck shoes! I saw them in a catalogue.
Not ugly waterproof kicks, or flippers
for me to flop about the deck on wet days,
or wear to the pond in the park. Not *duck, shoes!*
Nor shoes for a pet we might keep in a kennel,
it was late last night the duck was speaking of you,
but mallard heels in black, a duo of duckling heads
perched at the toes, leather upper, insole, sole.
Designer Chie Mihara, decidedly retro, with a snap
closure strap looped round the ankle, €300 a pair,
not each. Duck shoes. For me! Come on, just think,
just think of all the shoeless years! Those Cork stones
that rubbed a woman's sole to heck, the women still
barefooting it across Africa in search of a well,
and the years that were all too much about shoes,
bound lotus feet, Marie Antoinette, Imelda Marcos!
Think of the spectacle! The bird-bodied celebrity
chicks who had all Ireland in thrall with their Blahniks,
and the nine-year-old girl who stepped with both
of her feet onto a land mine last week –
but not us! And so when we lay down in our double
bed last night it was duck shoes I didn't wear
to tramp all over your sleek white back,
trace with a toe the seam of your cock,
raise my two legs like arms raised to cheer
over both of our grinning heads again, my dear.

Spawn

He took his children up to the wood
to collect spawn: it glooped moreishly
in punnets. They roared ecstasy at that and wilder
still when he explained they broke the law
to move the blobs at all. On the drive home
he constructed farces around handsome princes.

He painted the spawn a pool of fibreglass,
and his wife went wild at the fumes.
It's not I mind, she conceded in bed
when they'd made up, it's the barbecuing neighbours.
And when a bloated weeping slug was gobbled up by mobs
of tads, his daughter screeched like a teenage girl.
But everyone wanted their turn handling the first
shockingly lifelike pollywog.

His children left home, one a businesswoman,
one an artist-politician, and he retired.
He slipped out from under his wife's feet
to sit among frogs, his pool
of wilderness. They made music.
He cooed back, 'we're all in this together,' and,
'*les théories passent, le grenouille reste.*' He liked
that he could not tell if they were interested.

The Monster Surely

January, and the monster is still wearing your spectacles.
I have to read the daily specials to you from blackboards.

I want to ask you why you gave your spectacles to a monster.
But instead you get down on one knee and ask me to marry you.

Monstrous, his marshy breath steaming up your expensive spectacles.
I answer an ad for an eight-month-old coonhound.

That monster, I mutter, is pure spectacle for the neighbours.
And you can't walk the dog because you can't read the signposts.

I start waking at night to read the monster Ginsberg.
O monster for real feed my hunger for spectacle.

Say, let's get away from it all, get us a garden shed. Then
I make it with myself in your huge monstrous spectacles.

The Hotel

The deliberate mistakes in maps:
I swarm in the pool at Livingstone
while you smoked in the shade;
I caught the eye of a beautiful man.

Zambian, caretaker,
ascending down his ladder. I smile and arch.
I languish at him, preen. He sees.
When I pad off, all Brigitte,
he comes after. Calls. I waddle faster.

His weight on me a statistic
converted to a jerking digit,
imagination racked. What would I risk
for quick bliss?

Yours, certainly, but not my own death.
After that I insisted we swim at night.
I wake to it still:
the Southern Cross, the huge moon,
the enormous bat.

The rose on our watering can, our cats
parked ill-matched in the yard,

the man in the story on the ladder with the shears
who lopped the dolly's head off.

I wish I had a river

In bed, eyes closed,
he moved hands
over a dream-parade of girls
while she lay beneath, eyes cold,

thinking how a river would remain the same river
if its course reversed
or if it divided into separate streams and converged
somewhere else or H_2O was replaced with chocolate
but if water changed to concrete
and she hitch-hiked her way away
on the river it would be a road. After that

they'd tell each other
how love should be a lightsome thing,
not rooted deep in fertile soil, but
able to uncoil as need call – or cling.

Molly Bán

Two men slipped down a hole and found it:
massive, off-white, flirtatious, manifest,
a blasted albatross or a wedding dress
that had been dragged through Doolin and

hanged. It was there all along without us.
You should have seen it, and in the café,
the massive pavlova. I saw my sister write
in the guest book that the great stalactite

was a note in God's notebook.
It had no designs on a mate.

The second man's wife saw it a half-century later.
All that time it had grown like a growth inside her.
When she saw it she wept, for it seemed not to have aged.

Her hair was white lichen by then, a fretwork of veins,
hands a burren of lines, cunt a cave. Age accumulating
uselessly as calcium carbonate. One assumes

she loved the man – the story does not relate.

They've dubbed it the wet dishcloth in Doolin,
but you would have seen poor Molly Bán,
for they'd crooned her praises at the wake:

Tramping to her lover's flat, snared in a downfall,
she'd wound herself up in a sheet from the line
and he plugged her, taking her for a downy fowl –

truth be told I was relieved, for it wasn't the cob
she was marrying she was on the road to meet.

Before Doolin I had been in Connemara; dead
there was a good woman you had loved well
but I could hardly know. So I left you
there to grieve, I came away.
                              Wedding

sometimes seems a loveless woman feigning
love, who folds herself in between us – bony
arse, long hair, impossibly long limbs.
O love, we intone, passing between our two

sets of hands stones, echoes, precious metals,
who lifts the frills of your flippy skirt to expose
the slow-growing bony folds of a world
flirtatious, manifold, we cannot control:
                              Let us alone.

When the guide turns off his torch
it's still there. What's left unclear

is whether that's my ghost or its ghost
or your ghost – or hers, I suppose.

The Art of Losing

It's all, then, a slow accumulation:
a stone thickening with trilobites, a doll

acquiring layers of paint, the weight gained
with age. I travel lightly, but I stash

my treasure hoard somewhere. Wallpaper peels
to reveal pattern; my skin peels from skin;

I graze my shin and the pain is disproportionate.
Roald Dahl's talisman, glimmering on his desk,

was a ball of silver wrappers added
to each other over years, and I have seen

the same done with elastic bands for no
better reason than accumulation.

It's plain to see the real mystery:
why, with all I gather to me, I dwell

so often on the things I've shed. I could
easier list my losses, the denim

jackets, watches, dignity, perfectly
affable friends, than all the curiosities

I still keep in my cave hoard,
troved on shelves.

Unheimlich

1

The widower and his flock of sons locked up,
doused, drove away from that lit-
up house, not cocking back a glance. It shocked
me with its intensity of dwelling, a nomad clan's
determination to moonlight flit their own
haunting. I dreamed the building burned
about my spirit lugs, flames lapping
at porous skin, shriek of beam collapsing,
terror at my own translucency. I see through
the fire in my belly and lunge to leave with them,
am shackled to my post like a nag in heat,
swan-upped, lackeen, bracketed in a fixfax.

(It was a story
I first heard from my mother

at the portable typewriter,
setting up home

in burnt spaces between
one line and the next)

2

On the way home to wake you, Dublin
a pentimento, redbirds seagulls, squirrels
pigeons, clouds thunderheads. I dream
I'm the husband leaving his ghost,
hands haynish on the wheel, a life spent
making things kushti, horse sense.
I cannot make out how you stayed
in this town, selling houses, snorting coke,
until your heart burst, after I'd grown up
and left. I want to tell you: *asshole*.
All that you missed. Perhaps
you were trapped, beneath glass.
Perhaps
you were trepanning,
chewing for an-
aesthetic, saw it all
from where you started, spread-eagled
in sneachta, glittering
fish scales,
hospitable numnah, let it all have you,
settled in,
arms outstretched to a world –

Gadje, snow angel, bowerbird, Blanche.

Panopticon

Only don't, I beseech you, generalize too much in these
sympathies and tendernesses – remember that every life
is a special problem which is not yours but another's,
and content yourself with the terrible algebra of your own.

HENRY JAMES, in a letter to a friend

We are up to our pits in Sunday papers
when my father says that things never used to happen
when he was growing up. He means
the black crawly crawly Darfur fly, man
on a leash, girl with burns, crumpled machinery
at Inishowen; and he means Matthew,
who died last night at last of madness.
My father and I at the eye of the panopticon,
two of Prometheus' descendants, bound
at the centre of a shrinking globe. Sometimes
he used to turn the television off, newspapers
would grow angular holes
where bloodshed had been. Now it's I
want to fold cranes of the papers for him,
build bonfires of TV sets.
It circles us, the noise, all the same. When people ran
from the falling towers, they stopped
to buy cameras, stood
with their backs to the towers to watch
the cards fall over and over
on shop window screens. No wonder
that you with your too much of gentleness
wanted out, and we did not stop you.
Your friends expect to weigh forever
what we could have given
against what we could not change.
What kind of algebra would it take?
Matthew, love, I carry myself with care on Mondays.
I lie to hairdressers. I walk. I carry a notebook
to write down feelings

45

in case I need them again. I pretend
to be someone else at traffic lights. I stay clear
of mirrors, newspapers sometimes. I live
as best I can. I do the awful maths.

Silt Whisper

That summer one-eyed jacks were wild:
we learned new rules, left tea to brew.

Smoke stilled air. Leaves lay unturned.
Unemployment was another high.

I had been a storm in a polystyrene cup,
seeking scald, steam, instance, but now

we drew up lists; mapped out desire lines; skipped
interviews to collect blooms; paused before flight.

The only record of that time the silt of prophecy,
the memory of weight in our cupped hands.

For a short while we held the one breath:
I could never set it down.

Bluff

You walk with your hands
closed.
You do not remember
with your heart.

You will not solve it
that way, I want to tell you.
You will not remember I carried
my bag on my back across the field
to your house like a child. You carried
me up the stairs when I got there.

Clap your hands. See what you can find
in your pockets. Lie to hairdressers.
Communication is a marginal by-product; language
is a snowflake. Do you remember
when I closed my eyes and you led me
across the field? Let the exit
have you. Open your hands,
leave me there, run.

Polder

That was the summer men ceased
turning to leer me past and confirm
for their records my one side
was good as the other. At first

I asked why I'd ever thrown away
a day on jeans, wasted an evening
before the box in that, my short
passing-time. I thought of wedding,

a son who would consider me
lovely a breath longer: they had quit
straightening their ties and their spines
when I stepped, skirts hitched,

carefully into an elevator. By September
I'd learned to hitch my skirts further
up; I turned to watch men pass,
to see was one side as good as another.

Je me souviens

I recorded it all, the vast welkin,
beaver tails, unicyclists, each quirked
graffito, non-extinct elk, francophone,
wobbling fleck of poutine like jello.

We were circling thirty, sailed a rented
vehicle stacked with hair straighteners, anti-
perspirants, coconut M&M's and lip balm.
We all had passable boyfriends.

Adrift among accidents of translation
the natives hardly noticed, let alone
sanctioned or not-sanctioned our presence,
but sure we'd invaded, without a harped ensign

we'd taken the place. It wasn't the first time
but this time we'd hold fast, being three Dun-
drum women at the peak of our powers:
Carolyn Cummins, Ailbhe Darcy, Isabel O'Connor.

And then, I got to compose our letter
to the CEO of the World Empire:
Give in to our demands for Ulster
if you want Canada back in one piece.

Terminus

When Arnie sliced a transept from his own burgeoning arm
the inventor went loose all the way through.
You could see it in his face, clear as a dolly zoom,
that he would do anything the Terminator said:
and Arnie said he ought to quit inventing.

Even then – a boy joy-maddened with explosions,
the adrenal-squeezing soundtrack, my private crush
on Edward Furlong – I could pick holes in it.
Would topping one inventor really halt invention? Still,
it was a flick worth making the leap for.

Not yet unstoppable as Arnie,
I'm halted at Hardington, hemmed in outside Heathrow, doubting
my own innocence. The planes we'd hoped to cull
buzz overhead. We rally, sing
protest without Sarah Connor's conviction.

I'd half kneel to pray to the future wiser me:
Couldn't you send back a Terminator?
Not only would He lop the knees off those police cocks
picking round our squats, but take His pound
of flesh and lay it on the table:

How the machines, having what we've always dreamed –
the ability to fly to the high ground
when the ice caps dissolve –
take for themselves what's left of the world,
leaving nothing for us and the bystander animals –

But perhaps, as I've mentioned, it wouldn't matter what he said.

Swan Song

In the dark times
Will there also be singing?
Yes, there will also be singing
About the dark times.

BERTOLT BRECHT

I

When I used to span and busk my sails
I was a rare pen, black as a bassoon,
Blacker than basalt, a black ampersand,
Symphony in black minor.

But now she seems to float toward me:
An Aisling, light as a bird swing.

She leans to hand me the white feather:
I'm swan-upped, whoops, into the pot.

II

You crashed me to earth, ransacked me,
Shuddered the god in my gooseflesh.
My blank look, your red letter,
A complete and elegant theft.

III

I brood, yellow-peppered
In my own chawd-wine, sheepish, out
Of my element. Happed in you, feathers
Scales, wings fins, maw brackish.

You try to speak in pica, your claws kerns:
We lay a blotched ligature.

You've bitten off more than you can mew:
I've lined your throat with feathers.

52

Dark Looker

They rented the house by the quag for a fall.
He was writing a history of landfill;

she incubating, cooking kickshaw, the pair
of them chain-shot on the porch.

Locals warned them to beware the dark looker,
and science, he answered, is the view from nowhere.

She said nothing at that, only scored tight
little crescents in the skin of her grapefruit,

which oozed and was pellucid. Her far bits
grew horny, her top end bees-wisped.

*

Her feet have become claws completely
when she wakes birdalone one night: Tuesday,

though she's long lost track.
                 His hairless

head protrudes from the duvet, leathery
as her soles or an alligator pear.
                 She does it –
(*fuckit*)
splits it wide open with a spoon –

and slips in down the looming hole
with a flutter –
                 to huddle mobled, runcibled there –

holy molied, reduced to a head, roomed
of one's own –
                 and expands no further.

Catacombs

Dressed to slay, breathing smoke like liberty,
perhaps you thought you
could make that city yours
as long as you were there,
were surprised to find it riddled
with unmanageable tunnels
where death demanded of you

something pricey and uncertain.
Perhaps you thought if you did not pay the entrance fee
but wormed in of your own accord by night,
you could not be accused of tourism,
would not be a citizen,
would avoid the empty gaze of skulls,
leave without guilt if you chose.

Later, perhaps, when you tired of playing femme fatale
with a murky native of that place
you thought, since you had gazed the other way,
you could peel off those stockings and not be left
with criss-cross lines of red
prison fences
netting in your pale, clean-shaven legs.

The Room

(after Don Paterson's 'Bedfellows')

1

There are more ways to leave the room
than the door and the great bay-window,
but the exit may not take you.

The warren of links riddling your screen
with routes may all burrow back to your own catacomb.
The newspaper that unfolds like a trick,

predicting fortunes, might, laid out to be waked,
prove a map of tricks you've missed,
things you were too frightened to do

or to stop and you just kept walking –
round, in a loop. And the pelmetted dreams
you think you can lean back into,

taking the weight off, putting down time,
catnap you, frogmarch you, pigdog you
back to the zoo turned kangaroo court

where you are tried, found human,
found wanting, found making a dash
for the door, and sentenced back into the room.

2

There are no more ways to leave the room
than the window. No more shall I push
the door, that hard labour
that quickmarches me along the path of least resistance,
the road most taken, the exit into the mindless
masses of spectators. The wallpaper

along the stairs down to the street is yellow
and monstrous, the street sweats damp,
and in the hallway I have seen a rat turn
and answer my prayers with globe-eyed scorn
before waddling back into the shadows.
The shadows seething in corners only bide

their time, and every time I brave
that long walk down to the street
I am taking my life into my hands.

So I am making an executive decision. Set it down
that I left the room in the only way left to such a man:
by the window, arms outstretched, going forward.

Legacy

and finally, a screed for my children.
To you I leave the all-you-can-eat buffet,
the tall and grande coffee cups,
the sword swallower, the champion pork pie eater,
the television's unstinting hunger,
our own slow immigration,
and the night your mother wept silently,
not understanding I was too exhausted for desire.
Ñamma ñamma, my son, my daughter,
you have eaten all my love –
all you can eat.

To you I leave the language
I have learned with pain.
Reject the world as parataxis,
the quick syllepsis, the fall
into the egotistical sublime.
If the able stay indoors,
thugs will take over the agora.
Sing the descant chord,
sing it in a field, to open sky.
To you I leave it to win
each word over again, one word at a time –
gnamma gnamma.

To you I leave each full night's sleep.
At night, too tired to rest,
I have stroked your backs for wings.
There is a there there.
When a death happens in the family,
booking the flight will feel
like a doing something,
a Nyemi Nyemi.
Forgive your father
his age, his accent.
I leave you your perspective –

look back sometimes.
When you were smaller, more pliant,
we took you to see sights.
Once a tour guide declared,
'If you have a camera, you can take pictures.
If you don't, you can't. Simple as that.'
Numen. Numen. We had to hush you,
concerned you'd disturb the other visitors,
for you saw no reason not to laugh and laugh.
I leave you that simple as.

Caw Poem

Not atriums and ventricles that cup and pour
but a solitary magpie
beats cricked wings
against my ribcage walls:

oil-slippery, bug-ugly,
reflecting every colour and none,
playing I-Spy with the gleams of a mind,
singing hoarse and low:

you I caw to be a map   a metronome   a distance left to run
a red wheelbarrow beside white chickens   the lion for real
a rose by any other name   a word that has been won
a tangerine and spit the pips   days beyond the rhododendrons
a Huffy Henry hid the day
a madeleine   a dare to eat a peach   a pomegranate   a persimmon
a long cold drink of water   you
                    Chimborazo
                        Xanadu
                            Calloo
                                Callay
                            Weialala leia   la   lei

Edith said of the poet
that he was quite cracked
but that was where the light squeaked through.
I must have taken it as a clue.

I cocked my head
hopped a little, hopped a little closer,
love become a scrum, a scuffle,
a ruffle of feathers

as though I could
rifle through you,
plunder some bright thing,
learn to sing true.

Like a Ball

The playing field is a plane
inclined upward;
a bagatelle, a vertical
loom. The ball enters
play by means of the plunger.
Slam tilt, warp and weft.
Ignore the back glass, sing-
ing neon, sirens, sugar
gliders, blinking figures, all
of Gottlieb's fever. Mazy
as spinning Norns, web-spitting
spiders, Aran sweaters, the singular
mending stitch of a woman
of Srebrenica, what they tell you
isn't so.
      There is always a way
to go home, even if home
has shifted continents, sprouted
legs, speaks in steel-plated tongues,
draws the blood of innocent monsters.
I myself tilt, yawn, and keep rolling.

Funambulism

She's a loose cannon, all hook and bow echoes;
a high wire walker, tumbril, twirling a bumbershoot.
Cut you loose at the left ear, *makes
me want to join a revolution.*

I watched you go to her, a grin from eye to eye,
slacklining between two anchor points, palms out –
that one unfreckled part of you – here to Oz.
But she drank too much and now she's dead.
Makes me want to rock.

Position your centre of mass straight over your base
of support and come home to us, dear,
the ankle the pivot point.
Look forward and not at your feet.

Philippe Petit, between the two towers,
Maria Spelterini, or the Flying Wallendas.
She's canonical. She's canonical. She's canonical.

Observations on hearing she was leaving Australia for home

Her reports are all Web 2.0,
she is on the run.
A hall of mirrors such that
the source text is indeterminable.

*

She is keening today at a funeral for a stoat,
so she irons her red petticoat for a hood,
brushes her hair till it swoons, sets
her dandelion clock by the daytime moon,
all that jazz. Eats a hearty lunch, with wine,
pockets her black-handled knife, sets off,
her tale collected and catalogued.

*

On a blog about Britney:
So what if she lip-syncs?
The spectacle's the thing.

*

Holes for eyes cut in newspapers,
a full-length brown trenchcoat,
black, black Cadillac,
the shape of your heart.

*

I want to egg her on, set her
going like a flat black clock
with a MIDI alarm. But maybe
she knows something radial and whole.

*

Bones stacked, her body falls
into an unswerving column –
ears, shoulders, hips, ankles.

Buttocks relaxed, legs back,
belly strong, head raised.
She imagines someone pulls

a string from the back
of her head, allowing her chin
to fall level and her throat

to soften. She does not tuck
her tailbone. That's what I
imagine.

    *

Just as my phone lights up with her
position, my battery's dead.
~~I'm left with a memory~~
~~of what she might have~~

    *

Singing: How does an ant
work out how far it is back

to the nest? Glue stilts to its legs
before it strides out to the wilds;

take them off and it will walk
only part of the way back.

    *

Does someone go out and collect
the ants after the experiment is over?

    *

Something like:
knowledge is diasporic,
do not pass
Go.

A Report from the Mapparium, Boston

Between the trapeze and your feet,
for the sake of argument, we'll write it so,
there must have been a space where she was solitary

before she dropped. I read once how a woman
died in plastic surgery, hankering after
the more herself. Frightened, perhaps, of solitary,

she can't have dreamed how her husband
would push the heels of his hands hard
against his eyes at night when he was solitary

hoping to catch sight of her moving face
he's losing, or his eyes to bleed. Whisper at one end,
child at the other hears as if you both were solitary

and telling the secretest things. The sound
travels up and over. But stand in the middle
and you sound surround sound, utterly solitary.

Too, the drummer in a band I loved and never
knew has died in his sleep at thirty-four, for no
one reason. Each of these things is solitary.

Well I'm not gay, but he won me over, he'd sing
and I'd sing along. Now I turn to Jay sometimes and try
to breathe: night with or without him is solitary.

Elsewhere I read how Edison would hold a steel
ball in either hand as he considered these things.
If he fell to sleep, a ball, a solitary

ball would drop and he'd awake. Whatever came
into his mind just then, that was the answer
to the question, a kind of Solitaire.